GRaFfiti

Devotions for Girls

GRaFfiti

Devotions for Girls

J. DAVID SCHMIDT
with JOEY O'CONNOR

Fleming H. Revell
A Division of Baker Book House
Grand Rapids, Michigan 49516

© 1983 and 1998 by J. David Schmidt

Published by Fleming H. Revell
a division of Baker Book House Company
P.O. Box 6287, Grand Rapids, MI 49516-6287

Third printing, February 2000

Printed in the United States of America

Library of Congress Cataloging-in-Publication Data

Schmidt, J. David (John David)
    Graffiti : devotions for girls / J. David Schmidt ; with Joey O'Connor. — 2nd ed.
      p.   cm.
    Summary: Presents fifty-six readings with Bible verses and discussion questions on such topics as dating, parents, popularity, rejection, faith, temptation, and other aspects of daily life.
    ISBN 0-8007-5663-0
    1. Teenage girls—Prayer-books and devotions—English.
[1. Prayer books and devotions. 2. Christian life.] I. O'Connor, Joey, 1964– . II. Title.
BV4860.S35   1998
242'.633—dc21   98-5997

For current information about all releases from Baker Book House, visit our web site:
                  http://www.bakerbooks.com

Before you read this book, read this page.

You may be saying, "Here's another one of those dumb devotional books my mother buys for me."

But do you know what? Your mom, or whoever bought you this book, just might have finally come through for you.

This is one of those devotional books that doesn't require you to do a homework assignment every time you pick it up. You don't have to make any lists, write any poems, or say any cute prayers. All you have to do is grab your Bible, this book, and maybe a soft drink, and find a comfortable place to read.

God will do the rest, because this book has you in mind. It doesn't try to give easy answers to the big questions in your life.

What it does try to do is help you see that the Bible is not as heavy and complicated as you might think. I hope you will also see that it doesn't have to hurt to be a Christian.

Oh, yes, one more thing: For what it's worth, I've been where you are. I've fallen asleep trying to read my Bible, felt alone, and struggled over who to date. But if you're willing to give him a shot at it, God can and will help you in your life. I hope as you read this book you'll see what God can do for you.

J. David

Where It's At!

1 one

Leave Me Alone!

I wish everybody would get out of my face! My older brother is clueless about "social distance."

My little sister is an annoying little gnat—she's always storming into my room when I'm on the phone. And for just once, why can't my parents act normal? I wish I was a millionaire so I could buy my family a deserted island somewhere in the Pacific and send them there for, oh, let's say, a fifty-year vacation. Why can't everyone just leave me alone?

When the whole world is squeezing you with annoyances, pressures, expectations, demands, and irrational irritations, it's easy to feel harassed and helpless. Even wild mood swings are part of growing up as a teenager. Throw in the natural changes in your body chemistry, your monthly period, and the embarrassment that your body grows too fast or too slow in comparison to other girls. Remember your feelings for the gorgeous hunk sitting three rows over and two seats up in biology class, and don't forget to add that irritating brother. It's easy to feel overcome with dark moods, confusing emotions, and negative attitudes.

Throughout your life, you will experience times when your emotions and body chemistry are pulling you in opposite directions. You've probably already discovered that you can wake up some days with peculiar moods you can't explain. Your monthly period of aching cramps that are helped only by pain medicine and lying in a fetal position on your bed doesn't do much for your mental state. Trying to fit in at school, worrying if your clothes look good, peer pressure, and balancing the demands of school, friends, sports, homework, and parents, are serious challenges to sanity. **When you feel like screaming to everyone, "Just leave me alone!" try to remember what God says in Psalm 139:**

> God knows your thoughts before you think them; he knows when you wake up and when you lie down.
> When you were growing inside your mother, God was forming your body *and* your emotions.
> Whether you feel elated or depressed, God will be with you, guiding you, and holding you in his hand.

It should encourage you that, from the moment you were conceived until you die, God has *complete* knowledge of your life's joys and hurts. You will not always feel that God is in control. Strong feelings have a way of masking the truth. It becomes difficult to see what is real. Feelings change rapidly sometimes, leaving you feeling unsettled.

But your feelings, or lack of them, don't change the facts. God knows you, understands you, and is actively at work on your behalf. This is a promise you can count on, no matter how you feel. When you feel your emotions are out of control, take a minute to recall what Psalm 139 has promised.

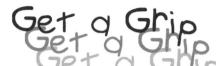

Get a Grip

Think about a recent situation or problem in which you felt depressed and moody.

How do you think God wants you to let him handle this kind of problem in the future?

What does Psalm 139 tell you about how special you are to God?

What *one thing* can you do when you feel overwhelmed by problems this week?

2 two HONORABLE Mention

My local newspaper covers high school sports in detail. Every week a special section called "Prep Extra" profiles the star athletes of the local high schools. Big photos, stats, and success stories cover individual athletes. Running backs, goalkeepers, forwards, cross-country runners, and tennis players are featured in full-length articles as if they were professional athletes. They are all in there—the stars that is.

Are you the kind of girl who always gets vague and unsatisfying recognition? You know the kind—awards like "Best Attitude," or "100 Percent Attendance at Practice," or "Most Likely to Succeed (on Another Planet)," or the ever-inspiring "Honorable Mention." Oh, to be smarter, stronger, taller, better built, or more beautiful. With such pressure to win and succeed, it's easy to wonder what you're *really* worth when you don't make the newspaper.

Your value as a person goes way beyond what you might feel you're worth. **Read what the Bible has to say about you in 1 John 4:9–19.** When you lack self-esteem, you carry some unnecessary baggage through life. Poor self-esteem makes you too concerned about someone else's good grades; you become terror-stricken giving a speech or being asked out. Your protective defenses cause you to hurt other people by the things you say.

Believing in yourself is important to personal growth. To believe in yourself, you must understand what is really valuable, not superficial values of TV and the movies.

The verses in 1 John say something important about your value. Your worth is measured in what God was willing to do to keep you out of hell. God declared your value when he acted to give you a better life while you're on earth. When the Almighty God of the universe does something for *you*, it's worth noting. In addition, he has given you talent and ability to do certain things well. In ways you never notice, he invests effort in your life. One thing to remember is that sin has a way of eroding your sense of worth. The more sin in your life, the easier it is *not* to believe in yourself.

If you are a Christian, God has drawn you out of a great crowd of people. Why? He saw in you a worthwhile person whom he loved and could use. This makes you very valuable. God's "Honorable Mention" list is different. Honor from God makes you an MVP.

Get a Grip

God has given every one of his followers special gifts, talents, and abilities. What has God given you?

Why do you always feel less valuable when you compare yourself to others?

What does 1 John 4:9–12 tell you about how much God values you?

three

3 Lighting Up

What female athlete do you admire the most? Is she a gymnast? A swimmer? Tennis player? Rock climber? How about a professional mountain bike rider? Whatever her sport, you can bet she hasn't achieved her success without plenty of hard work and discipline.

One obstacle that stands in the way for teenage girls who want to excel in sports or other activities is the pressure from "friends" to smoke cigarettes. In many movies today and on high school campuses, smoking is often seen as something cool. The "Just Say No" campaigns you remember from grade school go up in smoke (literally!) with the pressure to smoke.

Giving in to the pressure can get you into a whole lot more trouble than smoking a single cigarette. Just as practicing your favorite sport requires discipline, it takes discipline to follow God's ways instead of flowing with the stream to whatever your friends are doing.

God doesn't ask us to be disciplined people as a way of imposing useless rules on us. He knows that without some discipline we can never grow or refine our minds and our bodies.

Read in 1 Corinthians 9 Paul's thoughts on self-discipline. Without self-control and discipline, he implies, we cannot live with confidence.

Are you a Christian who struggles in your walk? The first thing to check is how regularly you read God's Word and talk to him. You really can't expect to remain close just by going to church on Sunday. Remember that Christianity is not just a set of rules. It's a relationship with the God of the universe, who cares very deeply about you. He wants to spend time with you alone, so you can get to know him better, much as you spend time getting to know a friend. But unless you discipline yourself to take that time regularly, you're hardly even in the race. By resisting peer pressure and living a disciplined, godly life, you won't see your relationship with God go up in smoke.

Name one area in your walk with God in which you would like to develop more discipline.

What one thing can you do this week to develop this discipline? Put it on the calendar—and check your success. Just do it!

4 four uncommon Sense

Stick a burrito into the microwave for a minute and what do you get? Dinner (or a mess). Channel surf up the numbers and where do you land? MTV, Discovery, VH1, your favorite show, or whatever. Type in a URL on the Internet. Zip . . . you're on someone else's server on the opposite side of the planet.

There are so many things we take for granted. We believe they will happen so confidently that we don't even think about it. Lots of things we do in a day require us to trust. *Trust* is one of those words some Christians throw around or use lightly. "Just trust God" sounds great, but it can be tough to do.

Jeremiah 17:5–8 has something to say about *where* to put your confidence. These verses say, *Trust in yourself* and you will *find yourself alone* when big decisions need answers. ("Where should I go to college?") You will *find yourself without roots* when temptations hit. ("I really didn't want to go that far with him, but somehow I didn't have the strength to stop.")

You will face lots of little but important decisions, and several big ones. How wisely you decide is directly related to whether you trust your common sense or God's. The Bible promises that, when we put our confidence in God, we become more *stable*. We *have less to worry about* when we face tough decisions.

Do you *trust* God by asking him to help you make good decisions? You know, God's got common sense. By simply asking him to help you with your decisions, you can have confidence that God will lead you right. Trusting God is like that. God is calling you to live according to some uncommon sense—his common sense.

Get a Grip

How will you seek God's wisdom for an important decision this week?

5 five

alt.culture

indie-
rockers • zines •
lollapalooza • nirvana • generation X • supermodels • designer drugs •
grunge rock • cyberspace • shaved heads • goatees •
Nike • piercing • no fear • Mortal Kombat • infantilization •
hackers • green marketing • LSD • Howard Stern • Patagonia •
wired • Oakley • gangsta rap • fat-free • snowboarding • muds

As great as it is to live in Western society, one force can be dangerous to your friendship with God. Popular culture has a major impact on how you think as a teenager. You can't live one day without getting blitzed with seductive messages that overemphasize beauty, sex, and making money. Popular culture will promise you everything—but deliver nothing. God says that he has a better way.

In their proper place, there is nothing wrong with beauty, sensuality, or pride in achievement. Out of place, they devastate a Christian.

First John 2:15–17 has some good thoughts on this. On the surface, these verses sound as if Christians shouldn't enjoy life, and if they do, God is not part of their lives. If you get hung up there you'll miss the real meaning. The writer of these verses seems to have had energetic, fun-loving, and "with-it" Christians in mind here. These verses are not a one-way ticket to boredom and a restricted lifestyle. Rather, they are strong warnings to stay *balanced* and to be aware of the *popular thought* in your culture.

We live in a society obsessed with physical beauty, sex, and material possessions. Sadly, all of these good things—which God has given to us—have been distorted and used wrongly. And the pressure is really on to think and behave like people who don't know God. The Lord wants to preserve you from the endless pursuit of what popular thought says is important.

There are plenty of good and decent things in modern culture, but it takes wisdom to spot and avoid things that are a waste of time. Let God shape your life, not popular culture.

Get a Grip

Today, God can help you
    realize that true beauty comes from inside a girl
    keep sex in proper balance in your life
    realize all achievements are blessings from
        him.
Think about God's promise in 1 John 2:15–17.
    What does this text mean in your life as you do
    his will?

6 six True Colors

Let's talk cosmetics. It used to be the choices were shades of pink, orange, and French Tip white. Now, Smog, Gangrene, Uzi Grey, Frostbite, Roach, and Asphalt can be yours for the low, low price of half your allowance. Urban Decay, the manufacturer of alternative colored lipsticks, nail polishes, and shadows, has created a mini-boom in trippy looking cosmetics that are getting more attention than the Clinique counter at Nordstrom's. Oh, and don't forget about Gash—it's blood red, and Shattered—lipstick the color of a green beer bottle.

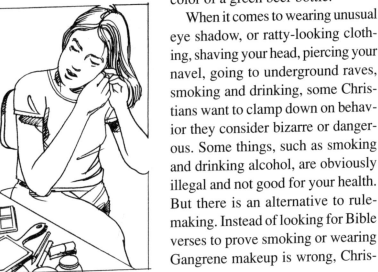

When it comes to wearing unusual eye shadow, or ratty-looking clothing, shaving your head, piercing your navel, going to underground raves, smoking and drinking, some Christians want to clamp down on behavior they consider bizarre or dangerous. Some things, such as smoking and drinking alcohol, are obviously illegal and not good for your health. But there is an alternative to rule-making. Instead of looking for Bible verses to prove smoking or wearing Gangrene makeup is wrong, Christians can find biblical principles for good decisions. **One of these is found in 1 Corinthians 6:12–20.**

Paul says that it's not really a question of rules. He knows he can do anything. The question is, what will he allow to control him? "I don't own my body," he implies, "it's God's." Therefore, I determine my behavior in terms of what pleases God, not what feels or looks good. Verses 19 and 20 provide the key: Your new life as a Christian was paid for by the death of God's only Son. One way you can show your thanks to God is to behave in a way that pleases him.

The question you need to ask about drinking or dancing is not, *Will my pastor approve?* or *Will my friends approve?* but, *Will God approve? Will this be pleasing to him?*

Get a Grip

What is the standard God wants you to use (in 1 Corinthians) to make decisions about what's best for you?

Here are four areas where this applies. As you think of activities in these areas, ask God to help you know if you're pleasing him.

1. What will I put in my body? (booze? junk food? caffeine? tobacco?)
2. What clothes and makeup will I put on my body?
3. Where will I take my body? (bars? movies? parties?)
4. With whom will I share my body?

7 seven

Second Chances

Have you ever said to yourself after majorly blowing it, "That's it! God's had enough. He can only be so patient. How many times will he forgive me? If I was a cat with nine lives, I'd still be roadkill a zillion times over." Do you ever wonder if God is sick of giving you second, third, fourth, and fifth chances? And even when you do ask God for forgiveness, you still feel guilty. Deep inside your heart, do you wonder if God cares about you anymore, or if he could ever use you for something important?

Read 1 Timothy 1:12–17. Consider this guy, Paul. Talk about an unlikely candidate for God's work. At one time he was directly responsible for killing Christians. He took it upon himself, before he believed in Christ, to track down Christians and have them murdered. But there is no sin too terrible for God to forgive. The Old Testament is full of stories of people who sinned against God—liars, egotists, cheaters, you name it. Yet, when they asked for forgiveness and continued following him, he forgave them and used their lives.

This doesn't mean we should sin just to prove God can use us. But since we all do sin, we need to ask him often to forgive and keep us on the right track. God isn't looking for super people. He's looking for people who will acknowledge their sins and turn to him. They're the only people he can use.

What about you? Do you believe God can clear the slate and use your life? God is bigger than any sin you could ever commit—just look at the people in the Bible and see what they did. The God who loves and forgives you is the God of second chances . . . and third and fourth and fifth . . . ad infinitum.

If God promises to forgive you, what is holding
you back from receiving his forgiveness today?
Think about an area in which you keep blowing it.
Ask for forgiveness and the grace to change.

8

eight

Guard Your Heart

While walking alone at night, have you gotten the feeling that someone was following you? Or do you feel uncomfortable standing at your locker next to a creepy-looking guy whose locker is right below yours? Do you ever fear your dad's temper? Is your neighborhood becoming a gang war zone? If you identify with any of these situations, you know what real fear is.

There are more subtle fears. Maybe you've been concerned over where your life is heading. You sometimes wonder if you'll ever have a boyfriend. Decisions can be overwhelming, even paralyzing. But there is hope and help for our fears.

The more afraid you get, the more you seem to feed the fear. **Take a moment to read Philippians 4.** Paul writes something that is difficult to swallow. "Don't worry about anything," he says (see Phil. 4:6). Right, Paul. Just how do you do that?

Verse 6 tells you how to guard your heart. Tell God your needs, and the peace of God, which is beyond our understanding, will guard your heart and your mind. That promise doesn't mean everything will be resolved immediately. What

Paul implies is that trusting God and doing what is right, true, pure, lovely, and good will somehow—we can't humanly explain how—allow the fear to settle.

The peace of God (v. 7) will come from the God of peace (v. 9). But it's something like driving. You aren't safe on the road when you just *read* the road signs. Safety comes as you *do* what they say. You need to trust God in order to find out that he will take care of you. Otherwise, you're just feeding your fear and trying to go it alone.

God promises to guard your heart by filling it with his peace.

Get a Grip

What is a specific area of your life where you need God's peace today? Talk it over with God, and ask him to give you his peace. Don't forget to thank him when he does.

nine

DO What I Did

Picture yourself twenty-five years from now. Maybe you're a mom and your teenage daughter is asking you all sorts of questions about love, sex, and dating. (Ridiculous? OK, but hang with me here!) You're trying to tell your daughter about how to choose a quality guy—not just any guy—to marry. You're talking about the importance *and* the benefits of waiting for marriage to have sexual intercourse. You're explaining the difference between infatuation, hormones, and authentic love. After your daughter fires question after question at you, all of a sudden the conversation stops. Your daughter looks you in the eye and asks you point-blank, "Mom, what did you do? Did you have sex before you were married?"

So what will *you* say? *Do what I did. Save yourself for your husband.* Or, *don't do what I did. I didn't wait, but I wish I had.*

What do you want to say to your daughter?

We live in sexually confusing times. As a teenager, you hear everything about your sexuality, your role as a woman, how you should handle relationships, and what kinds of sexual decisions you should make. It gets confusing. Voices, opinions, television, magazines, movies, church, friends, your parents—all have opinions. Where do you go to get good guidance about sex? The one source with a clear message about sexual decisions is the Bible. The Bible is very clear about God's thoughts on sex. He created sexuality and gave intimate sexual contact to humans as a gift. For good reasons, he restricted that gift to marriage. Hey, this isn't something most of us like to hear, because we all have drives to find sexual satisfaction. And things can seem so innocent and so right when you feel you're really in love.

Read Ephesians 5 for some helpful points about relationships and sex. First, we as Christians are called to be pure. That includes sexuality. Second, the husband is to love and care about his wife, as Christ patiently cares for those who walk with him. That's the model men are called to follow— and if you think it's an easy one, think about it some more. Third, marriage partners submit equally to each other—so neither partner rules over the other.

God set sex to be a part of marriage, not to spoil our fun, but because our lives are most stable and fulfilled if this intimate act is reserved for the committed love of the marriage vows. Those who go against the grain pay for it—in divorce, unhappy marriages, guilt, the feeling of being used, and venereal disease. Do you want to say to your children some day, "Do what I did," or "Don't do what I did"? You will begin to answer that question on your next date.

Get a Grip

In Western society it seems that women often set the limits of how intimate a relationship will become.

Even if you've made some poor sexual decisions in the past, what can you learn from past mistakes in order to obey God in the future?

ten

I Don't Have Anything to Wear!

It's ten o'clock on a Tuesday night. You're exhausted after hours of studying calculus, American history, and the subjunctive tense of thirty Spanish verbs. You have written a steaming essay on the subtleties of African coffee beans. You head to your closet to look for something to wear tomorrow, and the *real* homework begins.

You have a reputation to uphold—and every item in your closet is repulsive. With frustrated teenage girls everywhere, you scream, "I don't have anything to wear!"

It seems impossible that you just bought three new outfits last month.

Disappointment, depression, and discouragement are part of life. Maybe fashion isn't your only frustration. You've got your eye on the dress you're ready to buy for the winter dance, but no guy has his eye on you? Your parents fight all the time and you wonder if they're going to get divorced? When things go wrong in life and frustrations begin to pile up, it's easy to look inward at faults and shortcomings. If you do that too much, the result is self-pity.

Self-pity (the whiny-pouty-why-is-this-happening-to-me) is not a constructive way to deal with life's problems. There is no simple, three-step remedy to changing your self-pitying thought. **However, a way to begin is found in Psalm 103.**

Perhaps you expected to find some instructions about how to change your behavior. Maybe you were anticipating some secret formula. But the clue to beating self-pity found in these verses involves thanking God for who he is and what he's done for you.

Very often we are so preoccupied with our hang-ups and faults that we can't accomplish what we'd like. Then we feel even worse about ourselves. A good way to break this pattern is to acknowledge that we're stuck and unable to do all we want to do. Then we are free to turn our thoughts to God and his love for us. We get the focus off ourselves and our problems and onto God and his solutions.

You may not be able to solve your immediate fashion frustrations or the other problems in your life. What the Bible offers is a new perspective on what God thinks about you. You are still special to God, even when you don't have anything to wear.

Get a Grip

What do you have to remind yourself when you have nothing to wear?

Try this:

1. Read Psalm 103 again, aloud, as a prayer to God.
2. Make a list of ten things you can thank God for.
3. Thank him for his goodness.

eleven

Put It in Gear

Nobody said the Christian life would be easy. Sometimes we get the idea that, once we ask God into our life, problems immediately disappear. We expect God to answer every prayer like a waiter in a roadside diner. Sometimes Christians say silly things like, "You just need to have more faith. You don't pray enough." Or, "If you were really following God, then you wouldn't have these problems." Those are easy words for someone else to say, but they don't offer comfort and they don't fit what the Bible says. When things are tough, we don't need more faith. We need a tough faith, the faith we already have, put into action.

It doesn't take faith to sit down in a chair—you can see very well that the chair will hold you, and you'll be safe. Real faith is shown when you don't know what the results will be. When you follow God, even when you can't imagine things could work out, that's faith.

Read Hebrews 11 to see how some people displayed their faith in God despite incredible obstacles. Isn't it amazing how much faith Noah, Abraham, Sarah, and the others mentioned in this chapter had in God? They trusted him even when what they were told to do seemed ridiculous—even at the risk of being laughed at and ridiculed by their friends and relatives.

Some people were beaten to death, but they remained faithful to the God they believed in. They believed that God had something better for them, even when they didn't understand everything that happened to them.

This kind of faith isn't easy, and it doesn't come cheap. You may not be asked to suffer physically for knowing Christ personally. But you will have many opportunities to display faith in him, even when it doesn't seem to make complete sense. Marrying the right guy for you, choosing college, moving to a new town—in all these decisions and many more, you will need to have faith. What it really boils down to is believing that God knows better than you what is best for you. Do you believe that?

Get a Grip

What are you facing this week that is an *opportunity* for you to put your faith in God in gear? How might you do it?

twelve

12 Very **Cosmic**

Bio-sphere 2 was a two-year experiment in which eight human beings lived together in the Arizona desert enclosed in a three-acre, self-sustaining, glass-enclosed terrarium. This $200-million scientific "experiment" was designed to gain a greater understanding of the earth's ecological balance. But it was a complete failure. Biosphere 2 biodegraded into personality disputes, insect infestation, dangerous carbon dioxide levels, and an overgrowth of creeping vines. Nice way to spend $200 million, huh?

Do you ever wonder if God often looks down on earth and laughs at projects like Biosphere 2? Human beings, it seems, try to be smart . . . *almost too smart.* How smart do you figure God is? One of the words used to describe God's smarts is *omniscience.* That word simply means that God knows everything . . . including how to create the earth (Biosphere 1). I'm sure glad that God doesn't experiment with his creation as do human beings.

God's incredible knowledge actually is rather important to you. **To understand more about God's wisdom, read Hebrews 4:12–16.**

Everything you have ever said or done, the angry words meant to hurt your parents, your sexual decisions, what you say about someone you don't like, tests you cheated on—all are known to God.

Most of us do not live as if God knows all about us. We would probably live differently if we did. Someday you will have to give an explanation to God for *why* you lived the way you do. God can't stand sin in your life. He will work gently, by convicting you through his Word and your conscience. He will work firmly, through an event or disappointment to help you change an attitude or an action.

Because God is all-knowing, you can trust him with your life. Now that's smart living. God understands the absolute best route for you to take in life. That means he can handle the details.

Realizing that God is all-knowing should concern you and motivate you to live more carefully. But it should also help you breathe easier as you think about your future. There is no better place to be than the place where you must depend on an all-knowing God for direction. Involve God in your life. You'll never regret it. With God, your life will never be a wasted scientific effort in experimental living.

Get a Grip

Get a Grip

Why is it important to live according to God's wisdom? How can you remind yourself today of God's constant presence with you?

13

thirteen

All Fired Up

When you look into the mirror, what do you see? Do you see someone who wishes to be someone else? Do you see someone who is fired up to be the person God has created her to be?

Almost every teenager feels inadequate. There is unrealistic pressure to be beautiful, handsome, strong, sexy, studly, cool, athletic, and almost godlike in the uneasy quest to fit in. *Everyone is trying to fit in. Everyone is trying to be their best.*

"But what if I'm not beautiful or handsome or athletic or talented like everyone else?" you ask. "How can I accept myself as God made me when it seems like everyone else is so much better at everything than I am?"

The challenge is to discover how God has uniquely made and gifted you. **See what 1 Corinthians 12 has to say about getting fired up by understanding your unique talents and abilities.**

We all have gifts and talents that can be used, no matter how small they may seem to us. This passage describes how important it is for each person (part of the body) to do her thing, so that the entire body can function well. That's why there's no reason to play the comparison game. God doesn't rate one gift any better than another. And he doesn't ask us to function in ways we can't handle. He just asks that we give what we have to him to be used for his purposes. Many of us spend a lot of time and energy trying to be something we're not. When we don't accept ourselves, we make it difficult for God to show his power through us.

It's not God's plan for you to live a life of inadequacy and insecurity by feeling as if other people are better than you. You can live with passion and purpose by firing up for God all the gifts and abilities he has given you.

Get a Grip

List some talents or gifts you may have. Pick one of these that you particularly like and ask God to develop the quality in you for his service. But don't ask unless you really mean it.

What can you do today to put one of your God-given gifts into practice?

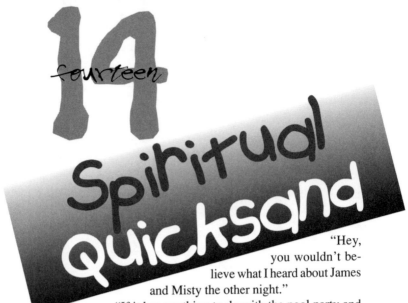

14
fourteen
Spiritual Quicksand

"Hey, you wouldn't believe what I heard about James and Misty the other night."

"If it has anything to do with the pool party and the Jacuzzi at Peggy's house, I don't want to hear anything about it. James just told me last week that he's on the student leadership team in his youth group. Just a month ago he was bragging about taking a purity pledge."

Have you heard a Monday morning conversation like this at your school lately? Throughout your life you will meet Christians who have different standards than you. Some Christians will *say* they have certain standards they live by, but their actions will show their *real* standards. Other Christians may be so strict that your standards (which seem pretty conservative to you) will appear loose to them. Some will say it doesn't really matter what we do or how we live since our sins will be forgiven. That line of thinking leads to spiritual quicksand. **Read Romans 6 for some insight about sin.** Apparently, some Christians in Rome assumed they could live any way they wanted and still be followers of Christ. They were betraying Christ by allowing sins to control them. And they were putting other things before God.

Sometimes we see sin clearly, because it's obvious. At other times, we kind of slide in—inch by inch—and before we know it, we've taken a big fall. Sexual sin often happens that way. It seems so innocent and right at the time. But impure behavior makes us slaves to sin. It's much more difficult to do the right thing the next time, once you've allowed yourself to go farther than you should have with a guy. That's how sin traps us and makes us slaves. Before we know it, we're sinking in our sin. The compromises of spiritual quicksand thinking can bury our conscience with the muck of self-deception.

One of Jesus' disciples compromised his life so much that he eventually destroyed his relationship with God and then himself. Judas betrayed Jesus for thirty shekels, or about $19.50. It seems crazy. Yet we daily betray God by living self-ishly, continuing in sinful behavior, and putting possessions or people before God. What about you? Don't allow little sins to suck you into the dangers of spiritual quicksand.

Follow God's standard for right living and what he says about sin. Even if you feel stuck in sin, God promises to help pull you out. You can be a slave to sin or live with freedom in Christ. The choice is yours.

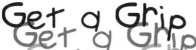

Get a Grip

How do teenagers who don't make specific dating and sexual standards get into trouble with their sexual decisions?

What are your standards?

What types of standards do you need to develop in other areas of your life today?

15 fifteen

Lean on Me

Will I ever receive a college volleyball scholarship? Do guys think I'm pretty? What if I don't pass my finals? Will I ever get married? Will I be pressured to drink at the prom? Am I fat? Am I a good enough Christian? What will happen if I lie on my college application? Am I destined to work at McDonald's the rest of my life?

Worry. Worry. Worry. Sometimes questions about the future become overwhelming. Worrying about your future is definitely not a fun experience, yet it can help your relationship with God. When we can't see the future clearly or when we're scared about the future, that's when we really learn to believe in, and depend on, God.

Take a moment to read Proverbs 16. You can make plans, the writer of these words says, but if you trust your life to the Lord, he will work his will despite your plans. Verse 3 carries an important message: Commit your works to the Lord, and your plans will be accomplished. If you've given your plans and future over to God, you don't have to be paranoid about making decisions that are unwise, immoral, or illegal. He doesn't have an impossible blueprint mapped out for your life so that you have to worry that you'll miss a turn in the road. The important thing is to allow him to control your life. Then, when tough decisions come, he'll guide or lead in ways you can't even imagine possible. This is a promise. God made it to you. And he never breaks a promise. That's something you can hang on to.

Get a Grip

Write down two or three specific worries you have. Give them to God to take care of and ask him to give you confidence that he will do it.

16
sixteen
Outta the Question

Your girlfriend grabs your arm in the hallway at school and whispers something into your ear. "No way," you laugh, pushing her against a locker. Surprised, your friend gets back in your face and says, "I swear it's true. He told me himself. You're crazy if you don't believe me. You're also dumb if you don't do something about it fast."

You just found out that the most handsome guy, who sits across from you in your third-period history class, has a crush on you. You've had your eye on him for a long time, too. You're flattered, but you're also frustrated. By the way he talks, what he talks about, and who he hangs out with, you know he's not a Christian. You, your friends, and even your Bible study leader have talked about it: Dating non-Christians is outta the question.

If you find this hard to take, you're not alone. As much as you may hate it, dating guys who don't personally know God is out. They are off limits—no good for you if you're serious about maintaining your walk with God.

Read what the Bible says about this subject in 2 Corinthians 6:14–18.

"How can one simple date with a non-Christian guy cause any hassle?" "No one falls in love by going to one football game together." "He needs me to tell him about the Lord."

That kind of statement is valid to a point. But you still have to come back to what the Bible says. The verses you read don't pull any punches. When it comes to dating and marriage there is no harmony between the believer and unbeliever. Some girls would say their values are the same as the guy's, but the bottom line remains: The Christian's purpose on earth is to please God, while the non-Christian's is to please himself or another person. You and he are going in two different directions.

If you have a relationship with a non-Christian guy, you need to stop and rethink where you are and where you are going with him. If doing the right thing is doing the tough thing, you can count on God to see you through. Waiting to find a Christian guy to date can be tough, but honoring God is worth the wait. Finding a Christian boyfriend, and someday marrying a Christian man who shares your Christian values and love for God, will definitely be worth the wait.

Get a Grip

Is God totally unrealistic about this issue? Why is it in your best interests to date someone who shares your love for God and Christian values?

Do you know someone whose relationship with God got messed up by dating a non-Christian?

What are the non-negotiable qualities of someone you'd like to date? Trust God to help you meet guys who fit.

17
seventeen

God@heaven.com

Ever get "bounced" by your friends? In e-mail and Internet terms, your message didn't get through. You got rejected. It's happened to all of us. You walk into the locker room after missing the game-winning point and your teammates sneer at you before heading to the showers. You pretend you don't give a rip, but deep inside you really do. Missing the shot was bad enough. Rejection by your friends is like pouring battery acid on a bleeding wound.

Sports may not be your thing. You may have just moved into a new city. You're trying to fit in at your new school and youth group. Or, you just may be a loner without any friends. How do you fit in when you're constantly left out? Do you ever wonder if you're going to face rejection and loneliness for the rest of your life? Will you always be left out? You know you need help, but where is it?

Read Jeremiah 29:11–13. Jeremiah felt discouraged and alone much of his life. God had given him the job of telling the Jewish nation to get its act together—to get back to worshiping God. Jeremiah needed a promise he could live by when he got lonely. God's promise came out like this:

1. God has plans for you, for good, not evil. That means you aren't alone, even when you feel alone. Someone smarter and stronger than you is looking out for your best interests.

2. God's plans will give you a future and hope. That doesn't mean hassle-free living. It means, whatever happens to you, God will bring good out of it.
3. God hears your prayers. Being part of a group at the time seems important. God knows your hurt or loneliness when that doesn't happen.
4. You can find God if you want to. The way to find him is simple enough—talk (pray) with him and look for him in the friendship of other people.

Loneliness is never fun, but knowing God is there and involved in your life can take the edge off your loneliness. By putting this promise to work in your life, you can work through your loneliness in a healthy way. Though God may seem distant and faraway in heaven, he is closer than you think. With God, you'll never get bounced.

Get a Grip

Take a minute right now and check in with God. He's ready to hear *everything* on your mind about your life.

18
eighteen
Verbal Virus

Have you heard about all the computer viruses slithering through cyberspace just waiting to zap all the precious data from your hard drive? Check out these pesky viruses. . . .

On the 13th of every month, *Chaos* counts 50 keystrokes, displays a message, and then hangs your computer. *Michelangelo* activates every March 6, the Renaissance artist's birthday. The *Cascade* virus rains letters and numbers from the top of your screen display. The *AntiEXE* virus causes your system to crash, the *Doomll.752* deletes your valuable data, and the *Nuclear* virus prints an antinuclear testing message on your Word documents. Whoa! Have you checked your antivirus software lately?

Just like a dangerous computer virus, our *words* can be a verbal virus. The Bible is packed with different types of conversations, as well as some advice on how we should talk. **Read James 3:1–12.**

You probably know the feeling of being cut to ribbons by someone's comments. Somehow, hearing them unleashes our own ability to strike back. The results often are a war of words and hurt feelings. The same thing can happen when we talk behind a person's back and spread rumors. It doesn't matter if a rumor is true or not, our words can wound and infect. Just as a computer virus is invisible, a verbal virus is also invisible, yet often lethal.

The Bible reminds us that words can and do hurt. As Christians we show our love for God and others by taking care how we use our tongues. Sharing our testimony at church on Sunday just doesn't demonstrate that God is working in us, if we were petty and gossiping on Thursday. This kind of hypocrisy screams of verbal viruses infecting our lives. Fortunately, God has an antivirus solution.

Get a Grip

What verbal virus downloaded from your mouth this week? Anybody you need to apologize to? Ask God to help you be sensitive to his voice so you can change the subject when friends start in on someone not present, and hear yourself when your conversation is hurting another person.

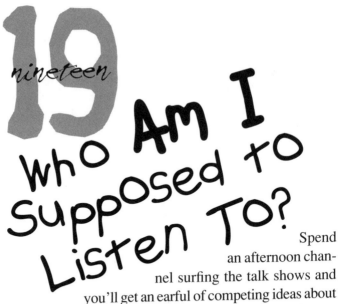

19

nineteen

Who Am I Supposed to Listen To?

Spend an afternoon channel surfing the talk shows and you'll get an earful of competing ideas about how a woman is supposed to earn respect. Oprah says one thing. Jenny Jones says another. Sally J. R. says something else. The studio audience blabs on and on. *Who are you supposed to listen to?*

Women are finally beginning to get a just share of opportunities and respect in our culture. You can't get respect from a television talk show or because someone says it's your due. Respect is something you have to earn. As a woman, you not only need self-respect, but you need the respect of those around you. Some women have their own ideas of how to be respected by men. **God has a different idea, which you should read in Philippians 2:3–11.**

Some women would say you earn the respect of men by

being aggressive
being as macho as they are in sports
giving yourself to them sexually

dressing well
beating them out for a job

The Bible sees it differently. You earn the respect of both men and women by treating them correctly. That means

being unselfish
living honestly, not to make a good impression
being humble
expressing interest in what others are doing
having the servant attitude of Christ

Notice the difference in the two lists; one builds up you and your accomplishments; the second (drawn from the Bible) builds up other people.

You can earn respect in life from those around you as you work to put them first.

Get a Grip

Respecting and thinking of others is God's way to earn respect. Pick someone in your life to serve today. Go serve them and see what happens!

20 twenty Supermodel Secrets

Cindy Crawford. Claudia Schiffer. Naomi Campbell. Christy Turlington. Elle McPherson. Kate Moss. Supermodels of the mid-1990s rank in the top tier of celebrities, right alongside rock and movie stars. From owning trendy restaurants to multimillion-dollar photo shoots to film deals with the top movie studios, supermodels have raised the standard of beauty, bucks, and brand-name fashion to never-before-seen levels. What girl hasn't, maybe just once, wished she was a supermodel?

The glamorous lifestyle of supermodels is being "marketed" to you almost every day through newspapers, movies, magazines, and TV. But how realistic is it all? And how happy and successful are these people? As a Christian teenage girl, how do you handle the unrealistic image of supermodels portrayed by the media today? How do you feel about other women's glamour when you don't feel too glamorous about yourself? What does the Bible say about glamour?

Read 1 Peter 3:3–6. At first these verses can make you mad or break your heart. The verses seem to say that glamour should not matter. But in today's world, how could it *not* matter? If you could read those verses in Greek, the language in which Peter wrote them, you would see that what concerned Peter is not that women are concerned about outer beauty, but rather that they expended such *time* and *energy* on appearance.

The pursuit of glamour takes valuable time from developing more important aspects of life. The Bible says the pursuit of inner beauty (and a gentle and quiet spirit) should be a higher priority.

Striving to be attractive is not wrong. The issue is balance between a gentle and quiet spirit and glamour. How much time do you spend each day cultivating a glamorous image? God can help you get and maintain a balance if you ask him for his help. You may never be a supermodel, but you can always know the special secret of God's love for you. God's love certainly may not be glamorous to the rest of this world, but it will provide for you a rich and deep inner beauty that will never fade.

Get a Grip

What is one character quality you want to develop and show this week?

21
twenty-one
The Love Connection

When
it comes to sex,
what does a guy really want
from a girl? Total resistance? In the sack
the first date? Some cat-and-mouse games for a while?
The answer to this question really depends on the guy. If a guy is really honest, he would admit sex is a large part of his thinking about girls. However, guys who are serious about their walk with God struggle to keep balanced viewpoints. Their viewpoints on what they really want should be (but aren't always) closer to what the Bible says.

For one quality you can develop that should be important to a guy, read Titus 2:1–8.

The one word that stands out is *self-control*. A lot of times girls leave it up to the guy to know when to stop kissing and touching. But these verses imply that women are to practice self-control just as much as guys.

Healthy relationships are built on responsible actions by both people in the relationship. This is not always easy to do, especially when your feelings are involved.

In their more honest moments, Christian guys will admit they need help from the girls they date to maintain their self-control. While slapping his hands so to speak might be painfully embarrassing at the time, you will strengthen your friendship in the long run.

So what does a guy really want from a girl when it comes to sex? Warmth and affection and romance—you bet. But, although at the moment it may not seem so, he also wants you to help him by demonstrating your self-control.

Get a Grip

Why would a guy find self-control in a girl appealing? Can you think of ways to gently show your date that the line has been reached?

22
twenty-two
Mental Makeover

What does a guy look for in a girl? A pretty face? Fun personality? Nice legs? Are you a loser if you don't have enough of what guys are looking for? Guys have definite opinions about what they like in a girl. Sometimes that can be difficult to handle if you come up short.

When it comes to wondering what a guy looks for in a girl, it's easy to get confused by wondering which is most important: inner beauty or outer beauty. Ask a hundred guys what they look for in a girl and you'll receive five hundred answers. What guys say is based on their moods, what they've eaten that day, and what type of deodorant they may or may not be wearing! To attract attention may require anything from a new style of clothes to a tattoo. And even then you can come up short. How can you get straight in your mind what is most important when dealing with the opposite sex?

Let's see what the Bible says are important qualities for a woman in Proverbs 31. These verses actually make up a poem that praises women. What's important to you, though, is that the qualities of a pretty woman can be acquired. You don't have to be born with them to become the kind of woman God has in mind. Helpful, trustworthy, energetic, competent, generous, well-liked, in touch with her world, respectful of God. All these are attributes you can acquire through some effort.

In his infinite understanding and care for you, God has made the qualities that make a woman beautiful available to *all* women.

Sensible Christian guys are looking for these qualities in a girl too.

It's easy to get mixed up over what really counts. A guy you know says one thing, your school friends another, and your mother a third. When you get confused about what really counts, refer back to Proverbs 31. As you allow God to change how you think about yourself in positive ways, you can put yourself closer to the right guys—who appreciate what God appreciates.

Before you attempt a physical makeover to attract a guy's attention, fix God's Word on your heart and mind for a mental makeover about what's really important.

Why do you think character qualities are far more important to God than physical beauty?

twenty-three

Best Friend

What do you look for in a friend? Someone who is loyal? Dependable? Willing to listen to you when you have a bad day? What about someone you can trust with your doubts, frustrations, worries, fears, and complaints? From the beginning, God's idea was to have you and others as his friends. If you listen to some Christians, it's easy to get fouled up on this and think God wants you to act more holy and be more spiritual. It's not true. God is looking to have a friend in you and to be a friend in return.

Read James 2:21–24. Abraham was a friend to God because of a very important fact—he *said* he would obey God and then *backed it up* with action. This same combination of believing in God and then acting as God's friend can make you a friend of God's too. Two things are worth remembering:

1. Faith isn't what you might think. "Just have more faith in God and you won't struggle with jealousy anymore." These kinds of statements just aren't true. Faith is the confidence we have that something we want is going to happen. You need

faith to believe in a God you can't see. Faith in God is the engine of your life. It motivates (moves) you to do right.

2. Faith isn't enough in life. You'll need to act right too. Right actions (driving the car of your life in the right direction) come from talking regularly with God (asking for directions), reading the Bible (the road map), and then just living (hitting the road).

Do you feel trapped by jealousy or something else in your life? Combining faith that God can help and right actions can get you started out of a rut. It takes time to get out of ruts and habits. We don't get into them overnight. But as you have faith in God and do your part to act right, you'll begin to see progress.

Get a Grip

Name one way God has demonstrated his faithfulness to you in the past. How can you respond today as God's friend?

24
twenty-four
Piercing the Heavens

OK, we all know people will pierce anything, *anything*, nowadays. It's *the* definitive statement of individuality you wear "quietly"— except that the piece in your tongue does seem to make an unusual "clinking" sound at dinner.

Body piercing definitely is an alternative fad. But it seems that in the search for self-identity and personal meaning, piercing your navel, nostril, or nipple only brings a limited amount of temporary attention from others. Then people move on to something more interesting or bizarre.

Prayer, on the other hand, gives you the opportunity to have God's complete and lasting attention. **If you'd like some new insights into this whole matter of prayer, read Romans 8:24–39.**

Praying is vital to your Christian growth. Because God looks at us as his friends, prayer becomes the way you and God communicate as friends. But let's get real for a moment. How can we talk to the God of the universe? Is it possible that he takes an interest in us? The Bible says yes. And it says here in Romans that when we pray, God's spirit helps bridge the communication gap between God and us. So when you pray, God hears your prayer correctly.

What is the bottom line? God promised to hear us when we pray, but he did not promise to answer our prayers according to our wishes. This doesn't seem fair or right, does it? Remember that God knows better than you do what is best for you, both in the short run and the long run (for example, whom you should marry).

Although it may be difficult sometimes, you'll be much better off in life if you take everything to God and then accept the results. Whether God says yes, no, or wait awhile to your prayer, you can be sure that he has your very best interests at heart. You don't have to pierce any part of your body to get the attention from God you long for. Your prayers always pierce the heavens.

Get a Grip

The Bible says nothing can separate us from God. Take a minute and connect with God. He'll pay close attention to everything you tell him.

25
twenty-five

Win at All Cost$?

Steffi Graf has had a sensational tennis career so far. Janet Evans has swum into gold medal after gold medal. Anika Sorensen has stacked up the golf victories. Million-dollar sponsorship deals. Front page coverage. Fame. World travel. Magazine shoots. Lots of money. *Ka-Ching! Ka-Ching!*

When you look at professional athletic contracts and sponsorship salaries, it's as clear as an Olympic swimming pool how important winning is. Defeat is no fun. It's an obstacle to anyone who wants to win. Should winning be that important? Should winning at all costs be the goal of everything you do? Are some victories more important than others? Are some battles not worth fighting? **Let's look at what the Bible says about winning at all costs in 2 Samuel 11.**

On the surface, David looked like a winner. He not only got away with sleeping with Bathsheba, but he also was able to cover up the plot to have her husband, Uriah, killed. But David blew it. He forgot that God saw what he had done. Eventually David's sins were exposed and what looked like a victorious cover-up turned into tragedy. David's honor was tarnished, his daughter raped, and his son killed. It was only after all this and David's humiliated repentance that there was any "victory" for David.

David and his family paid a big price for his desire to win at all costs. We should learn from this story that some defeats are not only more important than others, but that we often learn more from our defeats than our victories. A good test to see whether you have a "win at all costs" attitude is to ask yourself, *Will it matter a year from now?* Defeat can teach you a lot about life. Putting some of the smaller defeats of life into perspective will tame a hypercompetitive attitude.

David really messed up his life for a time. Yet, because his heart was right, God forgave him and built his character in the process. Maybe you've lost some big battles. You don't have to live forever with those defeats. Jesus said to come to him if you are weary (of defeat), and he will give you rest (Matt. 11:28). If you involve God in your struggles, he will turn defeats into constructive building blocks. You probably won't sign a multimillion-dollar contract like the famous women you see on television, but you can develop a Christ-like character that doesn't have to win at all costs.

Get a Grip

In what area of your life do you have a hard time accepting defeat? Any thoughts on what you think God feels about this?

26

twenty-six

Worth the Wait

If more than half a million teenagers can stand on the Mall in Washington, D.C., to pledge sexual abstinence, then you can do the same where you live. Since 1993, the True Love Waits campaign has had a tremendous influence in helping teenagers make positive sexual choices.

Each person seems to have an individual definition of *love*. Is it a feeling? A giddy emotion? A passionate sex scene like in the movies? Your challenge as a young person is to choose whose definition you will live by. If your mom and dad are divorced, you probably wonder if love and sex and marriage are really worth waiting for.

Read the well-known chapter in the Bible about love: 1 Corinthians 13. Paul wrote this letter to people who lived in the wild and crazy city of Corinth, where love was almost completely expressed by sex—and bizarre sex at that.

> Love is certainly a feeling, but the feelings are not the most important part of love. Love is also action and motivation.
> Love is patient and kind. It waits for the bathroom without grumbling.
> Love is loyal. It sticks up for a friend when she's not present to defend herself.

Love believes in someone. It encourages a friend to tell the truth.

Love expects the best from someone. It helps a date to be a gentleman.

Love defends others. It says something good about parents, even though everyone else cuts theirs down.

Love is not jealous. It compliments a brother on his good grades.

Love is not proud. It realizes certain talents are gifts, not rewards.

Love is not rude. It doesn't make fun of people who aren't as smart or pretty.

Love does not demand its own way. It would never say, "If you loved me, you'd sleep with me."

Love is all this and more. The highest definition is that God is love. Don't kid yourself into thinking something is love when it isn't. If you are wondering how well you love or if you are in love, try measuring your feelings against what the Bible says true love is. The results might surprise you. Even if you're not a virgin anymore, if you confess your sins to God, he is ready and willing to forgive you. He will give you the strength to make good decisions in the future.

Remember: True love does wait, and true love is worth waiting for.

Get a Grip

Have you made a definite decision about waiting for marriage to begin sexual intimacy? If so, tell someone you trust and ask them to hold you accountable.

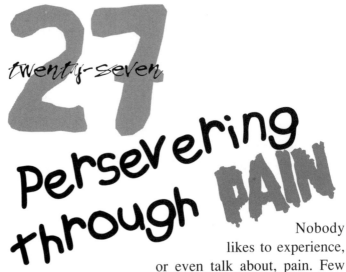

27

twenty-seven

Persevering through PAIN

Nobody likes to experience, or even talk about, pain. Few Christians know how to talk about their overwhelming feelings of anger, doubt, grief, depression, or brokenness when death and sudden catastrophes enter their lives. It's often easier to wear a fake smile and say that everything is okay instead of being vulnerable about feelings of loss.

In a broken world, pain and tragedy happen. People, sometimes people who are outwardly good, die young. The painful result is that the world of families and friends turns to hell. There are also all sorts of tragedies. A friend gets cut down in a drive-by shooting. A family friend contracts AIDS. A soccer player friend goes home one night after practice and hangs himself. Your dad walks out on your family for some girl at the office. Your best friend gets pregnant—then sneaks away to have an abortion. Your mom dies of cancer. Inside you fall apart. This can't be happening. You are left asking why.

Coping with the hurt and pain of life will be one of your toughest challenges. How can you persevere through the pain? How well do you cope? What strength do you draw on? **God's Word has some encouragement when you hurt; read Isa-**

iah 40:25–31. The last verse (31) is familiar to many Christians. Sometimes familiar verses lose their meaning or are used lightly. But a closer look at Isaiah 40:31 will tell you three things about how to cope when things go wrong in life:

1. We gain strength by waiting. Waiting on God means asking him to help, then watching to see how he will do it.
2. This verse is a promise. God never has and never will go back on a promise. But it is up to us to believe it.
3. The strength God gives helps us to do normal things like running and walking through life. God's strength also helps us to exceed what we thought possible ("fly like an eagle").

Ask God to help you. *Believe* he will. When something bad happens to you, your emotions get hurt. But to cope well, you don't need strong emotions. You need God to help you use your head to cope, not your feelings. You can persevere through the pains and hurts of life as you learn to lean on and trust in God.

Get a Grip

What kind of pain are you experiencing in your life right now?
If God wrote you a letter about what you are feeling, what do you think he'd say?

28

twenty-eight

Raising The Bar

How many people at your school went out for the high jump? Probably only a very few, if any. Most look at the high jump and say, "Forget it. There's no way my body could clear that bar." Not surprisingly, a lot of Christian teenagers feel the same about *holiness*.

You probably have a pretty good idea of what holiness is not. More difficult is the job of figuring out how holiness relates to your life. The very idea of holiness strikes "holy" terror in the hearts of most teenagers. Surely God is going to take away everything they love to do. Holiness seems to be something for grandmothers, preachers and priests, bizarre cult leaders, and old T-shirts. After all, doesn't God keep raising the bar? You think, "God is just waiting with a humongous checklist of things to eliminate from my life: no R-rated movies, no parties, no cruising, no dating, no, no, no, no. . . ."

To get a more accurate understanding of this whole idea of holiness, read 1 Peter 1:13–25. This is one of those spots in the Bible where the writer seemed to say something that is both confusing ("Be holy, because I am holy") and difficult to do. How can you *be* holy like God when you can't see him or talk to him face-to-face? Well, one of the great things about the Bible is that it rarely says something confusing without also providing some nearby explanation.

Several keys for being holy are found in the first part of what you just read in 1 Peter. It gives three things to do:

1. Prepare your minds for action. That means *think*. Use your head and avoid *in advance* those situations where you might be tempted to do wrong.
2. Be self-controlled. This is a tough one for everyone. It means to stop kissing your boyfriend *before* it gets too heavy. It means biting your tongue when your friends are saying negative things about someone you don't particularly like.
3. Don't conform to evil desires. Dig in and fight those attitudes or thoughts that you know hurt you and your walk with God.

God's holiness isn't like an eight-foot-high jump bar you have to clear on your own power. He has set a high standard to live by, but he doesn't keep raising the bar. His holiness in your life is based upon his understanding of what's best for us. He will supply the power—all you have to do is *let him work*.

Get a Grip

Name one way you need God's strength to help you pursue holiness today.

twenty-nine

29 Rules Are Rules

Not cool. Jack's expelled from junior high for bringing a broken air gun to school.

Apparently, his school has a "no guns" rule and anybody caught with a gun receives an automatic ticket out the door. Jack put the gun in his backpack, forgetting about the rule. He went to school but never took the gun out until he was on his way home. One kid saw it and told his mother about the gun. Mom complained to the principal. The principal called Jack's parents. Now Jack's out.

The principal didn't care that Jack forgot about the rule or that the gun never left the backpack or that it was broken. Rules are rules. *Seeya!*

Jack is a good kid. He's not a gangbanger, nor was he fearing for his life. Jack made a simple mistake that unfortunately had severe consequences. Jack learned the hard way that rules are rules.

We've talked about how God wants us to make holiness a priority in our lives. God wants us to be holy, not to make life a drag, but so we can enjoy the freedom that comes from following his laws and commands. When we decide to ignore or forget to follow his commands, we eventually discover that there are consequences for our decisions.

Take a minute and read James 1:1–18. Did you notice the pattern described in verses 14 and 15?

1. Our evil desires tempt us. ("I'd sure like to go drinking just once.")
2. If we give in to these desires, then we sin. (A six-pack later, you're plastered.)
3. Sin leads to death. (If you drive, it may be literal death. If you do make it home safely, you feel like you let down yourself, your parents, and God.)

Have you ever noticed how sin has a weird way of making you feel sick inside? Often when we sin, we suffer a deep disappointment in ourselves. This sense of disappointment comes from God. It is guilt and is designed by God to warn us when there is sin in our lives. You can pick any sin—drinking, anger, pride, lust, hatred, and so on. If you let it go long enough in your life, it will hurt you inside. The best way to describe that hurt is death.

Rules are rules. When we break God's rules, we only hurt ourselves. God gives us his Word so we will know how to become holy as he is holy.

Get a Grip

How do God's rules protect you from harm?
Take some time and think about his holiness in your life. It's the only thing in this world that will make you truly feel and be whole.

30
thirty

Yeah, Right!

"Because I said so!" Yeah, right, Mom and Dad . . . what is *that* supposed to mean? It is a poor use of the English language. Recall how your English teacher says to NEVER begin a sentence with the word *because*. In reference to the invitation to the party at John's house, the meaning is clear enough. "No, you can't go."

Does this sound like your communication with your parents? Ever heard any of these classics? "I really don't understand what you're saying," "Don't make me say it one more time," and the all-time favorite, "You're not going anywhere until that room is clean!"

Do parents take a class to learn this stuff? Do you know what? They are wrong to say them. But if you handle it emotionally, get mad or bitter, then things can get worse. The Bible has something to say about how we handle our anger.

Read what Ephesians 4:22–32 says about personal growth. The emphasis is on attitudes changing, truthfulness, and handling anger carefully. Actually, these verses are for you *and* your parents. When your parents say, "Because I said so," and you get ticked, you have a responsibility to go to them and tell them your feelings and work out the differences. They will grow from your openness. So will you. You will strengthen communication tremendously.

As you work on your attitude and go to bed mad less often, you'll find it easier to accept some of the strange things your parents say. With God's help you can have a good influence on your parents and do your part to make home a better place to live.

Get a Grip

Ask God to help you be honest with your parents and to give you the right attitude about talking to them.

Next time your parents say something that drives you nuts, what are *you* going to do that honors them, God, and you?

31

thirty-one

Don't Buy It

Despite everything you may see on MTV, hear on the radio, or read in your favorite 'zine, yours isn't the first generation to experience restlessness and hopelessness. You may feel cruddy about yourself, your family situation, your

lack of friends, the environment, and the world. There's lots of stuff going on to make you feel uneasy.

If you're a Christian, you may even feel like it's a sin to feel restless, insecure, or hopeless. Since the time of Jesus, many sincere Christians have experienced periods of restlessness and hopelessness. Even Thomas, one of Jesus' friends, felt this way. **Read about Thomas's restlessness in John 20:19–31.**

Like Thomas, we want hard, tangible proof that being a Christian is worth it. Jesus said to Thomas, "Don't be faithless any longer. Believe." Actually, believing in Jesus today is much harder than it was for Thomas. Computers and television have made us skeptical of the supernatural—of things we can't see and figure out. Not being able to figure something out leads to doubting, and doubting leads to restlessness.

The lyrics of *Smashing Pumpkins, Pearl Jam, Nine Inch Nails,* and *Alanis Morrisette* say a lot about restlessness, hopelessness, and despair. What solutions are they really offering, though? Listen to enough music and it becomes easy to believe that God has abandoned the earth. That's a lie not to buy.

Restlessness is a part of our culture. It will always be there as a force, pulling us away from school and church and family. Like rebellion, restlessness can only hurt you if you don't channel it into something constructive like a prayer to the Lord. If you get restless with being a Christian, take some time to talk to God. God is the Lord of every generation. Including yours.

Get a Grip

What are you feeling restless about today?
Jesus talked to Thomas about his restlessness.
Write down what Jesus would say to you about
receiving his peace for your life today.

No Sale!

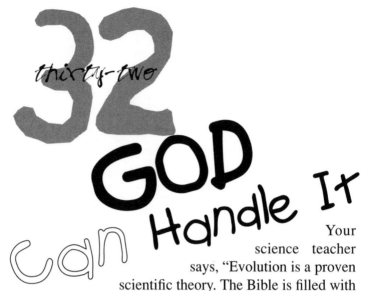

thirty-two

32

GOD Can Handle It

Your science teacher says, "Evolution is a proven scientific theory. The Bible is filled with mythical fairy tales about a creation story. It has stories to prove the existence of a so-called God."

One of your best friends says, "I can't understand how a loving God would let so many people, even children, suffer from starvation, war, and poverty."

Even Christians experience doubts about God. Does that mean your faith is doomed? Do your doubts mean that you don't love God? If there were some way to prove that Christianity is not real or that God isn't going to deliver on the heaven thing, you can bet a lot of people would live differently.

Do you ever wonder whether Christianity is worth it? If there really is a God who answers prayer? Doubts are part of the process of believing in God and taking him at his word. **The Bible has encouraging words about belief in God in Psalm 8:3–4 and Hebrews 1:1–3.**

When you have doubts, there are three things to think about:

1. It is extremely difficult to believe that all of the universe and especially the consistent order of things on earth came about without the intervention of a supreme intel-

72

ligence. The evidence is with the Christian, not the above science teacher. Consider, for example, the complexity of the human brain. Even scientists sometimes say that humans seem to be copies (images) of something not found on earth.

2. The Bible is unique. No other religious book has withstood such criticism, and only the critics are proven wrong. The Bible remains a best-seller. It defies the odds. Nothing gives cause to believe that this Book is not what it claims to be—the official writing and history of the supreme intelligent Being who claims to have created the heavens and earth.

3. Believing and practicing what is in this Book changes people's lives. Putting faith in the God/Man Jesus Christ who is written about in the Book changes murderers and liars. It frees people from guilt. It gives people a sense of purpose in life. Psychology can't do it, science can't. No other religion so thoroughly revolutionizes a person as believing in Jesus Christ.

Doubts are part of life. Even if you're feeling doomed when you doubt, God can handle your doubts.

There's no doubt about that.

Get a Grip

If you're doubting, take some time to recount all the big and little proofs you have that God is real.
Name one way God proved to you that he is real.

33
thirty-three

FA$T Ca$h

On a Wednesday afternoon in a poor neighborhood outside Miami, an armored truck overturned and spilled hundreds of thousands of dollars in cash and coins over the street. Residents scooped up every dollar, quarter, dime, nickel, and penny they could. Within twenty minutes, over $700,000 in cash and food stamps was missing. Women even took off their blouses, filling them with money and walking off in their bras. People claimed the overturned truck was a gift from God. Pennies from heaven. When a dozen police officers knocked on doors to recover the stolen money, the only thing people offered was blank stares and silence. Total turned in: zero.

Read Proverbs 22 and consider its advice about reputation. If a Brinks truck overturned in your neighborhood, what would you do? Go for the fast cash? Or, would you keep your reputation for having a good name? The Bible says here that you may be faced with the choice between riches and a good name. It's interesting that verse one sets up this choice. If a person's reputation is tarnished, it is most often because he or she didn't handle money correctly. But you may also have to choose a good reputation over a good time (sexually) or popularity (lying to cover for a friend).

This chapter makes it clear that a good name is worth more than money, a good time, or popularity. Sometimes Christians have used reputation as a club to whip people into line. "If you mess around on a date, you'll get a reputation." "If you don't tell the truth, you'll get a reputation."

People do know us by how we act, but the real reason for living correctly should be to please God, not fear of what others will say.

You can rebuild a tarnished reputation. God forgives and forgets your past mistakes. He wants to help you live right, so that you can rebuild or maintain a good name. When faced with the choice to go for fast cash or a good reputation, go for the second. In the long run, it's worth more than a truckload of cash.

Get a Grip

Why was it so easy for the people to rationalize their stealing by saying that the money was sent by God?
What do you try to justify?
In what way do you need God's help to make good choices today?

thirty-four
34
Slackers

In the mid-1990s, a soft drink manufacturer introduced a new soda. Labeled "OK Soda," this offbeat and strange-tasting drink was packaged in matte-gray cans that featured a couple of emotionless cartoon slackers on the outside. The marketing campaign promoted it with catchy slogans like "Don't think there has to be a reason for everything."

A 1-800-I-FEEL-OK hotline was even set up. Teenage callers could leave messages, listen to the snide and cynical remarks of other teenagers, and take personality tests on the hotline. Much to no one's surprise, OK Soda went flatter than carbonation on a hot summer day. So much for the slacker soda.

Life without Jesus Christ is like OK Soda—it looks like the real thing, but it's not. When Jesus Christ came into your life he changed you, turned your life around, and gave you hope and peace. God used other people to get the job done in your life.

If you are a Christian, you have an exciting message to share that can change the life of your family and friends. God's Word talks about the importance of sharing your life and the message of Jesus Christ with your friends and relatives. Being a Christian is so valuable. We have the privilege to share it.

Read Romans 10:1–15. Generally speaking, there are two types of Christians: "silent witnesses" and those who leave tracts in the washroom and hold evangelistic services at the bus stop. Neither extreme is appropriate all the time. The silent witnesses never try to share their new lives in Christ with others, and the *fanatics* turn people off. There is a middle ground.

Today, God needs people who know him and who are mature enough to say in public what they believe in private. Most Christian high school students can't share their faith in Christ with others because they fear being rejected or losing popularity. So they remain silent witnesses while their friends have abortions, get drunk, and endanger their lives. How do you break the silence? Here are some simple ideas:

1. You don't have to pray before every lunch, but a regular quiet prayer lets your friends know God is in your life.
2. Invite some friends to a Bible study. But be sure you have open discussion about what you read. Don't hold a church service.
3. If your church has a good youth group, invite your friends to an activity.
4. Ask your friends some questions about their beliefs in God. God can open up discussion among you and give you an opportunity to share your faith.

God doesn't need Christians who go around whacking people on the head with the Bible, but he doesn't need people who are indifferent either. God wants you to at least be willing to do and say something about your new life in Christ. Let the slackers stay on the soft drink can.

Get a Grip

Pick just one person you know who needs to know Jesus Christ. Ask God to give you an opportunity to share your faith with that person. He'll go with you.

thirty-five

God Talk

Christians have an insiders-only language. It's not commonly understood by the high school and middle school population across America today. If you've been in church or a youth group for any time now, you know what *God talk* is: spiritualized language that often means nothing but religious gibberish to those who don't speak it. God talk also may mean nothing to those who *do* speak it. God talk doesn't make anyone a better, stronger, faster, able-to-leap-church-steeples-in-a-single-bound, psalm-singing, spring-of-faith-type Christian.

Heard these buzzwords lately? *Born again. Filled with the Holy Spirit. Sanctified. Justified by faith.* These words or phrases can lose their meaning and become boring to you. So you know how an unbeliever will react—the great tune-out. As Christians we shouldn't tune out explanations and applications about sanctification, for instance. If we do we won't grow in understanding. Yet using this language around non-Christians can be a spiritualized code. The way some Christians talk can be a real pain.

The solution is found in 2 Timothy 2:14. You can trust the Bible to say it straight. There will always be "religious" people who are into God talk. It is useless to quarrel with them inwardly (inducing bad feelings toward the church or people) or outwardly (arguing or turning people off). You won't change them, but you can do something constructive. The Bible says to do two things: Do your best to be presentable (win your own battles with sin) before God, and be a person who knows how to handle God's Word (be clear and relevant in how you talk about God and religious things to other people).

You'll never get away from religious God talk or the Christians who use it. How you handle these people will be a test of your ability to accept others and to apply what you know about being a better person.

God talk gets in the way of people seeing Christ clearly. Identify some Christian expressions you use without thinking. Are there equivalents an uninitiated person can understand?

How can you demonstrate (and talk about) your faith today in an honest, authentic way?

thirty-six

Can I Trust God?

Do you have a hard time trusting others? The half of all teenagers in North America who've seen their parents get divorced are mostly skeptical of such words as trust, commitment, vow, promise, and loyalty. You may have a hard time trusting your friends as well. It doesn't take long to distrust a friend who broadcasts a secret more widely than NBC. Putting your trust in God can definitely be a scary step of faith too—especially if some important people in your life have let you down.

Can the Bible be trusted? When you think about it, Christians make big claims about the Bible. Christians say the writers of the Bible were inspired (directed in their thinking by the Holy Spirit) to write exactly what God wanted them to say. They also claim that we can trust God's Word to have no errors. That means we can trust its presentation of Christ and what he did.

Can you really trust a book that was finished almost two thousand years ago to be true and have any value in your life? **Read 2 Timothy 3:14–17 three times out loud.** One verse in this passage says, "All Scripture is God-breathed." What proof do we have that the Bible came from some powerful

God no one has ever seen? Here's something to think about: At least forty men, in thirty different occupations, wrote the Bible in three different languages over sixteen hundred years. In all, 807,367 words in the Bible work together in harmony to talk of one God, one devil, one heaven, one hell, and one way of salvation. The Bible has withstood wars, human criticism, and time to become the best-selling book in history.

But more than all of this, the best proof we have that God's Word is trustworthy is the fact that reading, applying, and believing it can change our lives. Because what is in the Bible are God's thoughts and insights on how to make it on earth, it links us to a loving God. Many religions have a "holy book," but no religion has a book like the Bible, which, when believed and applied, can be of such hope and help. History proves that when people take God's Word seriously, it works. Hey, how about your Bible? Is it working for you?

The mistakes of others can make it difficult for you to trust God and his Word—but not impossible. What one step of faith is God asking you to take to show that you trust him?

thirty-seven

Good Advice

How many times have you heard parents say ridiculous things that are supposed to help but don't even relate to your life? "When I was a kid. . . ." How would they like it if you stormed around the house wanting them to do things differently because, "When I was a toddler, this is how things were. . . . When I was in third grade, we did things this way. . . ." They'd probably shake their heads in amazement, just as you do now. What about when they ground you for walking in the door ten minutes late? *Grounded for being ten minutes late? . . . I'm calling my lawyer!*

Handling adults or parents is no small task for a teenager. Parents seem to have such out-of-date attitudes. They get hung up over little things like ten minutes or a messy room. The rules they want you to live by went out with hula hoops.

What's the best way to handle your parents, or any adult for that matter? **The Bible has some good advice in Ephesians 6:1–4.** This is a good passage to talk about with your mom or dad. There's something in it for both your folks and you. You'll notice that the Bible says that fathers should not exasperate their children. If you're feeling exasperated, you need to take the initiative and talk to your parents. Often teenagers have trouble with adults because of poor communication, not difference of opinion.

The important thing to remember is that God asks you to honor and respect your mom and dad, even when you disagree with them. Believe it or not, your folks have twice as much experience at living as you do. They've seen their own mistakes and hurts, and they want to help you avoid them. Don't let a disagreement over a movie, curfew, or choice of friends stand between you and your parents. Next time you have a hassle with them, whether you live with one parent or two, remember that God wants you to honor and obey them, not because "that's just the way it is," but because God has your best interest in mind. He provided adult guidance so that "it may go well with you" (Exod. 20:12).

Get a Grip

In what areas can you show more responsibility and so earn your parents' trust?

If problems with your parents run deep and seem to be unresolvable, is there a pastor or other mature Christian from whom you can get counsel?

38

thirty-eight

The Zit Zone

I have a mega problem. I don't go a day without a zit. They're everywhere. What's causing them? How can I make them stop? When I wake up in the morning, it looks like my face was up all night making pimples. How can I put an end to the annoying night shift?

What's the fastest way to get an ugly red zit to take a hike?

Cyberspace has zits . . . *a whole web site dedicated to zits.* Amazing. You can download all sorts of information on whiteheads, blackheads, megazyborg zits, and those infamous "right-before-a-hot-date-third-eye-Cyclops-dead-center-on-your-forehead" zits from the OXY–5 web site (www.oxyzone.com). As you can tell from the above students' questions, waking up in the morning and discovering your face is in the zit zone causes severe adolescent desperation. If fighting zits and acne is a daily problem, you probably wonder whether God is playing some sadistic joke on you. Like many other teenagers, you're not alone in asking, "God, are you listening to me? Are you there for me on the stuff that tanks me?" The Bible says, God is there for us—and the way God helps us is through the Holy Spirit. **Read John 15:26–16:15.**

The Holy Spirit is tough for a lot of Christians (even adults) to figure out. Our modern culture with its emphasis on logical thought, practicality, and technology leaves little room for a supernatural being like the Holy Spirit. Many young people get uncomfortable when there's any discussion about the Holy Spirit. For some reason, it just seems too far-out to deal with. And the church doesn't help much when it depicts the Holy Spirit as a mystical ghost who helps superspiritual people. Nothing is more untrue.

God knew that people flounder because they cannot see God. So the Lord provided a *Comforter*, a *Counselor inside us.*

The Holy Spirit acts with our consciences, warning of attitudes or actions that will hurt us, or comforting us when we hurt. It is a mystery *how* God works in people who know him personally. The Bible says the world can't accept this mystery. This is a danger too for Christians, who can be influenced by the world's thinking to believe the Holy Spirit isn't in them or is unimportant.

If you have asked God to forgive you of your sins through the death of Jesus Christ, and you are walking with him as Lord, God's Spirit is in you. This world will do whatever it can to discredit the Holy Spirit and his work in your life. Though your zits may vanish sooner or later, the Holy Spirit promises to remain always.

Name a way you sensed the Holy Spirit at work in your life.

Ask God to help you understand how the Holy Spirit is inside every true Christian. Ask God to help you depend on, not ignore, the Spirit's help.

thirty-nine

Gut Feelings

Guilt.
You know what it
feels like. Real guilt is that paralyzing, acid-churning, sickening feeling in
the pit of your stomach when you know you've done
something wrong. The longer you avoid dealing with the
guilt—that gut feeling that God is tugging on your heart—the
worse it gets. Stealing. Lying. Cheating. Premarital sex. Whatever you've done, your guilt isn't going to go away. Unless,
of course, you decide to do something about it.

It would be untrue to say that doing what you know is wrong
doesn't feel good at first—or that it isn't fun. But if you have
truly accepted Christ into your heart, God's Spirit within you
is hurt. It's as if he's been watching all along, and since he's
an integral part of you, you feel uneasy over your sin.

Read Psalm 32. This psalm of David brings home what
happens when we delay talking with God about sin. David
pours out his thoughts in verses 3 and 4—his unconfessed sin
had consequences. Once he admitted this, he knew God had
forgiven him. He could once again have a good relationship
with God. When you've hurt someone by something you've

said or done, don't you both feel an awkwardness that continues to get worse the longer you both ignore it?

The same is true in your relationship with God. If you keep ignoring what you know is separating you from him it will only strain the relationship, and you will feel distant from God. If you feel a wall has been erected between you and God, he is not the one who is responsible. Try talking to him about it, much as you'd talk to a close friend. He wants to share your sorrow and your fear. If you continue to separate yourself from him through unconfessed sin, you're hurting yourself and you're also hurting God.

Get a Grip

Reflect on your relationship with God. Is everything straight between you and God, or are you trying to hide guilty gut feelings from him?
Why do you think God allows you to feel those guilty gut feelings when you sin?

40 forty
Burnt Out

"I can't believe John calls himself a Christian," Denise snaps. "Did you see how drunk he was at Kim's house last Friday night? I liked him because I thought he was different than everyone else. He takes the concept of hypocrite to new levels. He's so inconsistent."

What are you supposed to say?

When was the last time someone else's less-than-Christian behavior created an uncomfortable conversation for you? You've been telling a friend about Christ, when you're smacked upside the head with the hypocrisy of someone else in your youth group. You witnessed someone who claims to be a Christian acting the opposite of the teachings of Christ. Maybe you've even thought in disgust, "If that's what a Christian is, forget it." Do you ever feel that other people's actions are burning out your relationship with God? If so, you're not alone.

Take a moment to read 1 Corinthians 3. Back when these words were written, some people in the church were rallying behind personalities—Christian superstars—and forgetting that the Christian faith rests on belief in God, not people. There have always been, and will always be, people in the church who claim to be Christians but don't live the life they profess. Sometimes they're even Christian leaders, like the religious leaders in Christ's time, the Pharisees.

None of us is perfect; we're all hypocrites in that we don't consistently live the God-dependence and purity of an authentic Christian lifestyle. We don't have to be perfect to be accepted by God. In fact, we need to admit our imperfections.

Keeping your eyes on people is one of the quickest ways to burn out on Christianity. Somehow it won't make much sense to someday stand before God and whine, "But God, there were so many hypocrites in the church!" He'll probably agree wholeheartedly and then ask the piercing question: "But what about you? I never asked you to put your faith in people, but in me."

What about you? Are you allowing other people to distance you from God? Are you confusing the wisdom of men with the power of God? Don't let the actions of others burn out your relationship with God. Stay focused on him, not others.

Get a Grip

Why is it so easy to look at other people's weaknesses instead of our own?

What can you do to focus on Jesus?

41 Body Surfing

It seemed like a pretty good plan at the time. You were thinking about which college you want to attend so you decided to get your history and chemistry grades up. So you've been studying a little extra. But you also wanted to make a relay team so you've been practicing a little longer. You've just come from track practice, an English paper is due, and *now* your sister wants you to go shopping. Help! I can't take any more!

Balance is a key to understanding our limitations and learning to say no. Without balance, gymnasts break their routine, wars start, people get the flu, fires ignite, banks get robbed. Balance insures quality, peace, and good health in every area of life.

Balance is not often talked about among Christians. Yet the Bible is one long record of God working to bring balance into the lives of people.

Buried in the New Testament is a phenomenal little verse of Scripture, Luke 2:52. You'll notice this verse divides the life of Jesus into four parts. He grew in

wisdom (mentally)   favor with God (spiritually)
stature (physically)   favor with men (socially)

Jesus, as a person, grew in normal ways. And because Jesus is a model for our lives, the verse makes a good measuring stick for personal growth. Your spiritual, physical, mental, and social growth are important to God. Over the next devotions we'll look at the importance of balance in each of these areas. Remember that God is committed to balance in your life just as he was in the growth of Jesus.

More than making you obey rules, God wants you to maintain balance in your life. Like body surfing, maintaining balance can be difficult when all you're doing is trying to keep your head above water. As you look at different areas of your life, remember that the love of God is an incredibly strong foundation on which to build a balanced life.

Get a Grip

What two or three things lead to imbalance in your life right now?
How can Jesus' example of a balanced life help you to grow?

42
forty-two
Mental Hula Hoops

Memory Fuel. Fast Blast. Energy Elicksure. Mind Mix. These are some of the "smart drinks." *Nootropics,* the mixing of drugs and nutrients to produce memory and intelligence in the human mind, is another trendy and expensive way to stretch the mind.

Popular at dance clubs, these drinks are mixed by savvy entrepreneurs who have an eye on making a buck by blending smart drugs with juices and amino acids. The results are questionable—no new Einsteins yet. Critics say these drinks give nothing more than a caffeine rush. James McGaugh, director of the Center for the Neurobiology of Learning and Memory at the University of California at Irvine, said, "These smart drugs are nothing more than a hula hoop for the mind."

You don't have to drink anything to improve the intelligence God has given you. God is concerned with *what you put into your mind,* and also *what you think.*

Read Philippians 4:4–9. If you could read this in the original language of the New Testament—Greek—you would see that these verses encourage you to think good thoughts, and let those thoughts shape your *attitudes*. That's because what we think has a big impact on *how* we act.

Thinking correctly is a vital part of being a balanced person. Remember that Luke 2:52 said Jesus grew in wisdom, as well as physically. Jesus could never have done what he did unless he developed and used his mind correctly.

Do you want to be smart? Maybe you're getting good grades already, and you can hold your own in most any conversation with an adult. That is not what the Bible calls true wisdom. The Bible says respect for God is the beginning of wisdom. And this respect isn't related to how smart you are. It's something anyone can have.

In Philippians we get practical guidance on what to think about. This kind of thinking can keep you balanced, so that your mind doesn't become a garbage can for the latest thing the world is pushing. Garbage in, garbage out. Your mind is worth more, both to God and to you.

Get a Grip

What is one particular struggle you have right now, that you need God's *wisdom*—his way of thinking—to handle?

43

forty-three

Jesus unplugged

Would Jesus play a guitar if he was on earth today? Order pepperoni on his pizza? Go to the mall? Hang out with "marginal" people?

To find out what Jesus was really like, read Luke 5:17–32. This story shows two sides of Jesus. Jesus had power from God to heal people, and he did. But he was *very human,* right down to eating dinner. What is most important here is *who* Jesus ate dinner with. The Bible says that the pious Jews of the day (Pharisees) complained about who Jesus joined for lunch. These guys couldn't understand that Jesus was interested in giving such people—tax collectors, prostitutes, thieves—a new life.

Sometimes our picture of Jesus is one-sided. The simple (and mysterious) fact is that Jesus was human. He had friends, including many who did not believe as he did. What does this mean to you?

This takes balance. It matters *who* your friends are. You can't go through life just hanging out with Christians, nor can you remain consistent if you have strong friendships with those who are rebelling against God. Any adult who cautions you about your friends is right. We have already stressed the importance of dating Christians. The key is balance.

Be a person of conviction when you are with friends who don't know God. If they put you down, then your friendship isn't as important as you think. When you do things with your friends who don't know God, do safe things in neutral places. Their influence is stronger than you are, no matter what you think.

Friendships are important in life. Choose yours carefully and be careful what you do with them. You'll save yourself a lot of hassles.

Get a Grip

Finish the sentence: "The one thing I'm getting pressure from friends to do, which I need God to help me avoid, is . . ."

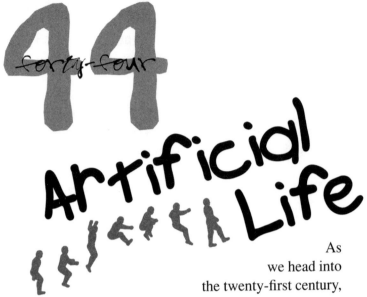

44

forty-four

Artificial Life

As we head into the twenty-first century, we'll hear more about artificial life and artificial intelligence—computers programmed to mimic the fundamental processes and systems of living beings. This new field involves such wild concepts as robots, fuzzy logic, and nanotechnology (repeat *nanotechnology* five times as fast as you can).

Artificial life has severe limits. It will never be able to duplicate the spiritual side of our lives. Artificial life may be an interesting topic to discuss and explore, but it can't give us eternal life. If we ever hope to be everything that God has created us to be, we need to learn how to balance the physical, social, mental, and spiritual aspects of our lives.

In Mark 12:28–34 Jesus gave two commands that can act as spiritual life keys:

Love God with all your heart, soul, mind, and strength.
Love your neighbor as much as yourself.

Wrapped up in these two phrases is a spiritually balanced life. Let's take a closer look:

Love God with all your heart (emotions), soul (beliefs), mind (mentally), and strength (body). All the aspects we have been talking about—physical, mental, and now spiritual—are here. The way to be balanced spiritually is to bring all of you into the process of loving God. That doesn't turn you into a religious fanatic who can only eat, sleep, breathe, and talk religion. God takes what we dedicate to him and points it at the real world where we live. He sees you as a whole person, not a "soul."

Love your neighbor as yourself. Here is the social side of us. God expects us to spend time with all types of people and to show love for them all, including our families.

As you seek after the eternal life God has for you in Jesus Christ, spiritual balance will come in your life. Be patient with yourself and God. As you work to apply these commands and to stay balanced in the other areas of your life, God promises to help in the process. You won't have to rely on a computer for artificial life. You can depend on the Source.

Get a Grip

What is a practical way to love God with all of your heart, soul, mind, and strength today?

---

45 forty-five

The Mask

In the movie *The Mask*, Jim Carrey's pea-green face, ultra-bright teeth, mile-long tongue, and googly eyeballs hid who he really was. He went through his days hiding. We wear masks to do the same thing.

To varying degrees, we all wear masks. We hide behind them with our real feelings and thoughts. Masks generally do more harm than good. God's perfect plan is to free you to be yourself—all the time. Unfortunately, sin has altered God's perfect plan, so we struggle with masks and disguise the truth. **Ephesians 4:17–32 has something helpful to say about masks.**

Masks can come in many shapes. People try to act smarter, richer, or more popular than they really are.

> If you get turned down for a date but tell your friends it doesn't matter—that's wearing a mask.
> If you go out with your friends to do something that you feel inside is wrong—that's wearing a mask.

Masks can hide our convictions, feelings, personalities, and Christianity from others. Are you lying to others by wearing a mask? The Bible says to stop lying to each other. That is a call to start today to be honest with yourself and others. You may need a little practice at first, especially if you've grown dependent on some mask. Ask God to help you.

The more honest you are with others about the real you, the more you will feel like a whole person. And you won't have to worry about your face turning green or anyone stepping on your tongue.

Get a Grip

What kinds of masks do you sometimes wear?
Some masks also hide you from yourself. Those
   may be particularly hard to spot.
Are there masks that would feel soooo good to take
   off?

46 forty-six

Happy or Holy?

God wants me to be happy. This is just one of the many myths of modern-day Christianity. Another myth is that God will answer every and any prayer—*prayers for a new girlfriend or boyfriend . . . prayers for an "A" on the test you didn't study for . . . prayers for more money so you can buy the right kind of cool clothing to stay in style with everyone else.* The list goes on and on. We sometimes think God's sole reason for existing is to keep us happy. Despite what we or many other people may think, God does not run and fetch for our amusement. The story of Jonah is a perfect example. **Take time to read the short Book of Jonah.**

Anyone with even a nodding acquaintance with the Bible has heard how Jonah disobeyed God and was thrown into the sea and swallowed by a great fish. The reason he disobeyed was that God sent him to warn a people he absolutely hated. God told him to tell the people in the city of Nineveh that they would be destroyed because of their sin. It was not an easy thing to do. Often in our lives doing the right thing is not easy or comfortable.

Jonah should have felt good after the people listened to him and turned from their sin. Instead, he was ticked. He felt so mad he wanted to die. He wanted to nuke the Ninevites. Jonah didn't understand why God was being kind to them. He didn't notice God's kindness to him. God wanted Jonah to trust him in all things. We don't know at the end of the story whether Jonah learned anything from his experience. He must have, since he or another prophet wrote it down for us.

What about you? Are you willing to do what you know God wants you to, even when the results don't go your way? You may have to go the extra mile with your parents for a while, without seeing them ease up on you. It may mean giving up friends who are bad influences on you, even without any friends in sight to take their place. In the long run it will always pay off to do what God's Word says. However, in the short run it helps to remember that walking with God doesn't mean we'll always be happy or comfortable. Jonah certainly wasn't happy with everything God told him to do, but ultimately, Jonah evidently decided that following God's plan for holiness was best.

If you want true, lasting joy and not temporary happiness, set your heart on holiness.

Get a Grip

Ask God to help you today with your point of view. Following God may not always make you happy. What is a practical way you can practice holiness today?

47
forty-seven

keeping His Promise

If convenience stores are open 24 hours a day, 365 days a year, why do they have locks on the door?

Why do mattresses have warning labels? Do you *really* get in trouble if you pull them off?

If nothing sticks to Teflon, then how does Teflon stick to the pan?

Why do girls always go to the bathroom in groups, and why do guys communicate in grunts and shrugs?

Why do parents act like zombies when you ask to borrow ten bucks?

These are perplexing questions, just a few of the many things in this world that you and I can't understand. As Christians, there are also a lot of things we don't understand about God. In fact, we often have a one-sided view of God. Since we can never understand totally what he's about, the most we can do is look at who he is through ways he has interacted with people in the Bible, and how he has revealed himself to us personally. But even then, it's hard to understand how he can judge our sin on one hand and be a loving Father on the other. Most of us know what it's like to be punished or judged, but few of us have really experienced pure, unconditional love.

Read Romans 8:35–39 and its list of things that can't separate us from God's love. Not life, not death, not angels, not the powers of hell, not your fears, not your worries, not even if you're flying or in a submarine.

Did you notice that "sin" is not included on the list? Though a Christian cannot "lose" her salvation, sin does separate us from the closeness God desires. We are not separated from the love of God. If you feel alone or have failed in a certain area, remember this promise—nothing can separate you from the love of God. You can count on him to forgive you and to be with you today and forever. In this confusing world, the one thing you can trust in and understand is that God always keeps his promises. His doors are always open, and there are no locks.

Get a Grip

Name a particular promise God has kept in your life. Does that memory help in down times, when God seems to be on vacation? Is he, or did you back away from him?

48

forty-eight

The Price of Popularity

A friend goes out for the football team, a club, or cheerleading squad. All of a sudden your friend is a totally different person. He doesn't return your phone calls. She gives vague, hesitant answers about her plans for the weekend. She doesn't sit with you at lunch anymore; she's sitting with her new crew of "popular" friends. Now your friend is popular, and you're a half-eaten bologna sandwich.

If you're feeling alone and ignored because of a former friend's newfound popularity, or if you're popular and want to know how to keep things balanced, read how popularity changed the way some people behaved in Jesus' time. Popularity problems have been around for a long time. As you probably know, the price of popularity can be high. **Read John 12:37–50.**

In the case of the Jewish leaders, respect and praise mattered more than what they believed. It mattered so much that they compromised their honesty. Pushing for popularity can do the same thing to you. It's good to have friends, but whenever finding friends and looking for their praise takes your focus off important things in life, then things have gone too far.

In the same way, if you are tempted to compromise to stay popular, your life is out of balance. Balance is the key, and God can help you get it and maintain it. But the price of balance is not cheap. Check the balance in your life. Fewer activities, attending fewer parties, and learning to be comfortable alone may be in order.

Friendships and the respect of people are important. Having the friendship and respect of God is more important. There's always a cost for popularity, but popularity comes and goes. Friendship with God can last forever. What it costs is all of you.

Get a Grip

Wanting to be liked is normal. Not staying true to God and yourself just to be popular—isn't normal. Have you set compromise limits? What are you just *not* going to give up to be popular?

49 forty-nine

X Games

ESPN came up with a radical alternative to the Olympic Games. The X Games are the insanest adrenaline-pumping, extreme sports you can imagine: skateboarding, skysurfing, sport climbing, street luge racing, bungee jumping (yes, you can now actually make money by tying rubber bands to your feet and plunging hundreds of feet), barefoot water-ski jumping, bicycle half-pipe competitions. . . .

The X Games have a definite, rebellious edge to them. These extreme sports are radical. They push the limits. They challenge the conventional sports. Many of these sports reflect the hard-core, push-the-limits, rebellious nature of men and women. Like the X Games, sometimes we want to be different, unique, playing by our own rules, rebelling against God. We want to find a new alternative.

Rebellion is in everyone. After you become a Christian, rebellion still raises its head. **To see how God**

looks at rebellion, read the story of a lost son in Luke 15:11–32. Rebellion has consequences. The lost son spent his money, got quite hungry, and felt so low he went and took a job feeding pigs. But the story doesn't end there. The son made a choice to come back, not knowing exactly how his family would respond. His smart choice to live differently paid off.

And the choice to leave a rebellious spirit or attitude behind will pay off for you too. God is not going to condemn you for wrestling with rebellion. He is vitally concerned about whether you channel rebellion into something constructive.

Throughout your life you will co-exist with rebellion. But as you let God control your life more and more, you will begin to see ways in which you can use that desire for change for something useful. The church needs people who can channel their desire for change into new music, drama, strong leadership, and relevant thinking.

Rebellion in your life can be an asset or a liability. It all depends on whom you go to extremes for, yourself or God. It all depends on whether you want to play games with God.

Get a Grip

Rebellion against God hurts both you and him. Think about one area of your life where you feel like going your own way—not God's. Share it with a Christian friend who can pray for you and hold you accountable.

50

High-Tech Truth

Have you noticed how major companies use spiritual themes for their print and television ad campaigns? IBM has produced television ads showing Hindu monks meditating. The caption at the bottom of the screen makes a double reference to the Hindu symbol and the Lotus Software Company: "IBM and Lotus in spiritual harmony." Another ad has depicted a couple giddy Italian nuns talking about their recent exploits surfing the net. *So spiritually tubular!*

Though companies and ad agencies may use spiritual words or concepts, they are presenting their version of spiritual truth—not God's. God presents in the Bible real *truth* for living, not just information.

Paul wrote a letter to a young friend, Timothy, which talked about how to handle the information in our lives. **Read 2 Timothy 3.** These verses are really appropriate for our day. What is interesting about this letter to Timothy is that it is probably one of the last letters Paul wrote. Just think. Paul used one of his last letters to a friend to tell him that God's Word is important and useful in helping us live our lives.

There is something to learn from this. God's Word is important in our lives. Without it, especially in today's information-packed world, we have little or no hope of making sense out of life. There's just too much out there to try to figure out.

How regularly are you reading God's Word? It's not how much you read or how long you think about it that counts. But are you arming your mind with its truth? The chances of you keeping your head together are slim unless you are regularly exposed to reality and truth. God's Word can help you in life. If your Bible reading is irregular or only occasional, you need to reevaluate just how important the Bible is to you. Set a reasonable goal for yourself so you read more this week than last. You'll find that God's Word can give you the help you need.

The Bible may not be high tech—but it is high touch. It's God's preferred and best way to get clear information to you on how to live a life that pleases him.

Get a Grip

Use a daily planner to schedule, for one month, five minutes several times each week to read the Bible. Quantity of time isn't so important as the opportunity to really focus on what God says. If you start this discipline, you will come to enjoy and anticipate it.

51

fifty-one

A Blockbuster

Gripping, hand-to-hand, bloody battle scenes. Illicit sex. Intrigue, betrayal, and conspiracy. Families divided by jealousy, lies, and government coups. Sorcery, witchcraft, and demons.

And you thought the Bible was boring! The latest Hollywood blockbuster has nothing on the amazing, action-packed adventures found in God's Word. "Well, what about special effects?" you ask. *Water flowing out of a solid rock. Fire from heaven consuming animal sacrifices. Raging seas stilled in a second. A small girl rising from the dead.* How's that for starters?

You may feel guilty and think something's wrong with your walk with God if the Bible doesn't grab you as did the latest thriller every time you read it. The Bible is packed with exciting stories, but once you've read them a few times, don't feel weird if you get bored. It's normal to go through times when the Bible reads like any other book.

For more insight on what to do when your Bible reading just isn't working, read Deuteronomy 6:1–9. It's not very obvious at first, but in this chapter is an angle on the problem of dry Bible reading. You'll notice God told the Jewish people to impress his commands on their children, to talk about them everywhere, to tie them to their hands (or memorize them), and to write them on the door (communicate them to others). What was the point of all this? Two things are important.

First, God seems to be saying that variety is good when it comes to learning his Word. There is no set way to have your devotions. If you are sharper in the morning, then read in the morning. If you want to read out loud to a friend or someone in your family, that's okay too. There is no law that says you have to read the Bible a certain way or at a certain time of the day. God encourages variety.

Second, there's an old saying: "This Book [the Bible] will keep you from sin; sin will keep you from this Book." God's Word is valuable and can correct our bad thinking and instruct us on how to live a holy life in today's crazy world. But sin can keep us from getting the most from the Bible.

Next time your Bible reading gets boring, ask God to help you. Check your life out. Then try some variety. If you are serious about being a Christian, you can't ignore God's Word. It can be your lifeline to God's best for your life. Unlike Hollywood's blockbuster hits, the Bible has stood the test of thousands of years.

How is your Bible study going now? When it's hard to read or understand, ask God to give you one thing to help you. He will.

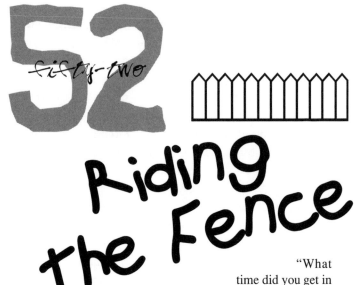

52

fifty-two

Riding the Fence

"What time did you get in last night?" your dad asks you as you sit down at the breakfast table on a Saturday morning.

"Oh, a little after eleven," you say in a confident voice. You hope the conversation will stop here.

"Eleven, huh? That's funny. I was up until midnight reading and I never heard you come in."

"Well, you see, when I said, 'after eleven,' what I really meant was. . . ."

You know he's got you. Cancel your plans for the rest of the weekend. You're busted!

Certain things just do not mix in life. The Bible talks about two attitudes that are on opposite sides of the fence. If you want to be all that God has designed you to be, there's no way you can be riding the fence between his way and the world's way. **Read about these two attitudes in James 4:1–17.**

The Bible is clear—being friends with the evil pleasures of the world makes you an enemy of God. This is not easy or fun to hear. But it is true.

Some of the most unhappy and frustrated Christians are those who try to party on Friday and Saturday nights and then show up for church on Sunday mornings. It just doesn't work. Christianity requires our concentrated commitment. It is not designed for people who are undecided about its value. This doesn't mean we have to be reclusive and hide away from the world. It doesn't mean that life has to be one long prayer meeting. It *does* mean that the value system of a Christian is different. Having a good time, dressing well, and partying with lots of friends can be part of a Christian's life, but not the *same* place as in the life of someone who doesn't know the Lord. The Christian's motivation, attitude, and actions are going in a different direction than those of the world. This is especially true when it comes to the sorts of things that give pleasure.

Are you trying to have a good time God's way *and* the world's way? It won't work. Put your whole commitment into doing things God's way, and you'll see some of the pieces of your life start to fit together. Riding the fence isn't worth it. Do you want to live with frustration or peace?

Get a Grip

In what ways do you sometimes ride the fence between God's way and the world's way?

53

~~fifty-three~~

She shoots,
she scores!

your Score

What is your batting average when it comes to temptation? Are you winning more than you're losing? Losing more than you're winning? Maybe things have gotten gray. To be honest, you haven't noticed fighting a temptation for some time. Sometimes temptation is very clear. Temptations to shoplift or have sex or damage others' property are easy to spot as wrong. Other times, rights and wrongs aren't so clearly defined. How do you handle gray-area temptation when it comes?

Take a moment and read 1 Corinthians 10:1–14. Sometimes God doesn't have to discipline us for sin—we discipline and even punish ourselves. At the time, it's easier to give in and do what we want, but we usually pay for it. Embarrassment, guilt, hurt, broken relationships, even death can result when we give in to temptation.

When Jesus died on the cross, he broke the *power* of sin in your life. How this works is still a mystery. The important thing to remember is that, while the *power* of sin in your life was broken by Jesus' dying, you will still sin. No one will ever die having completely beaten sin. This doesn't mean you should give up and give in to temptation. Rather, God wants to help you get your batting average up and give in to temptation less and less.

Ask God to help you hear his voice clearly when you are being tempted. You may not hear a real voice, but God can guide your thoughts and conscience so that you will find the way of escape he promised.

Get a Grip

What makes it so difficult to call on God when you are tempted?

What can you do to discern God's will in a gray area?

54
fifty-four

Losing My Religion

Stupid rituals."Do's and don'ts." Hypocrisy. These are a few of the reasons some teenagers give for rejecting a relationship with Jesus Christ. Many young people think following Jesus means that they have to become "religious." They think God is a kind of demented Santa Claus, a cosmic and ruthless tyrant who keeps a daily tally on what they do or don't do.

Well, God does keep a record of our lives, but not in the way you and I commonly think. **To find out exactly what kind of spiritual scorecard God keeps, read Psalm 103:9–18 and Luke 10:20.**

These verses in Psalms and Luke tell you what God *doesn't* put on your record—your sins. The Bible says God doesn't bear a grudge or remain angry forever. He has moved our sin away from us as far as east is from west—in other words, a distance that defies measurement. You may have noticed that God moves the sin away from *you*. Why? Because God loves you as a person but hates the sin in your life. Separating you from your sin by more miles than you can measure guarantees God will never see you and your sin together. It guarantees complete forgiveness. The record kept is whether your name is registered as a citizen of heaven. And that's up to you.

Such concepts as your name recorded in heaven seem off-the-wall, particularly in our world, which is so in tune with what can be seen and sensually experienced. But the concept *is* real. Your whole hope of living after you die is tied to this concept. The Bible has made it clear that when people come to Christ for forgiveness of sins their names are recorded in heaven.

Do you have confidence that your name is recorded in God's book of life in heaven? Or have you been playing religious games? Maybe you've been faking your Christianity for so long that you've fooled even yourself. Maybe it's time for you to lose your "religion" by developing a real relationship with Jesus. Knowing God personally is your only hope for a meaningful life and living forever. He's waiting to hear from you. Lose your religion and gain a relationship that will last forever.

Get a Grip

How does it make you feel knowing that God
throws all your sins as far as east is from west?
If you know that you've been playing games with
God or not taking the sin in your life seriously,
go ahead and talk to God about it right now.

55
fifty-five

It's NOT My Job!

"If I hear you moan and groan, whine or complain one more time," your mom snaps at you, her glasses steaming with a menacing mist, "you're going to be in big trouble! I'm sick and tired of your attitude about helping around this house!"

"But it's not my job. I took out the trash last week. It's that little, lazy doofus's turn to do something around here for once." You cast a squinting-evil-eyes glare at your lower-life-form younger sister.

"I don't care if it's her week to take out the trash. . . . I asked YOU to do it!"

"And what if I don't?"

Ooouummph . . . Dooonn't aaaask thaaaat question!

Too late.

Chores are a part of living. Always have been. Always will be. What is your attitude about chores? **Read what the Bible says about attitude in 1 Peter 3:10–17.** These verses give you a formula for a happy attitude toward life:

Keep control of your tongue. (Do your chores without complaining.)

Don't tell lies. (Are they *really* done?)

Turn away from evil. (Be honest. Do them when you are told to.)

Live in peace, even if you have to chase it. (Accept the criticism and the praise when it comes.)

It takes a lot of energy to keep a house going and in order. Sometimes parents can get so busy that they assign chores without thinking about your tests or date. The same formula that will help you handle the chores will also help you work out the differences with your folks. By sitting down and being reasonable (controlling your tongue and doing your best to keep peace), you will demonstrate an attitude that is pleasing to your parents and to God.

Get a Grip

Why is a good attitude about serving others (yes, even your family) pleasing to God?

56 fifty-six

Next Steps

The
Christian life is
often compared to a long
journey filled with roadblocks, setbacks,
peaceful rest stops, bumpy roads, and uphill climbs.
Along this road we travel with Christ, the rock-strewn path
before us is solid but seldom smooth. Maybe that's why I enjoy
hiking in the mountains so much—traveling steep, difficult,
narrow trails provides a physically challenging example of a
deeper, inner reality of what it means to follow Christ each
day. One thing long hikes will reveal is which muscles or tendons are out of shape or weak.

The Achilles tendon in your lower leg gets its name from
the Greek soldier who was supposedly immune to enemy
wounds except in his heel, the anchor point for this tendon.
An arrow struck him down—you guessed it—in the heel. If
you've ever pulled that tendon in sports you know how
Achilles felt. It is a painful injury.

Like muscles and tendons, we all have areas of weakness
in our lives that can be spiritually injured if we're not careful
where we step. We have "Achilles tendons" in other areas of
our lives too. For some reason everyone's personality is predisposed to a besetting sin or repeated failure in one area of
his or her life. **Read Romans 7:15–25 for some insight into
protecting and strengthening these vulnerable areas.**

Sometimes we get the impression that heroes in the Bible never struggled in life as we do. These verses should put that myth to rest. Paul gets down to some honest, gut-level communication. Whatever it was, Paul's struggle went with him. Like all who want to please God with a holy life, he found himself sometimes beaten by sin in his life.

As long as we live, we struggle with sin. As you get older, what tempts you might change. Whatever it is, its power in your life was broken when Christ died on the cross. But you will still sin. With Paul, we have to turn to Christ to rescue us.

As a Christian, you have important choices to make about what trails to travel. Use your head and stay out of situations where you are easily tempted. Call on God often for help. Remember that Jesus is walking beside you, in front of you, and behind you. All along the way, his Spirit will comfort you, encourage you, prod you when you're tired, and give you the rest you need when you feel like you can't take another step.

Walking with Jesus isn't always easy. But there's one thing you can count on—by staying close to him you can be sure that he'll help you where you're weak. His strength is "perfect" for anything you face today and the rest of your life.

Your weaknesses are opportunities for you to depend on God, if you turn to him for help.
How might God use the worst tragedy or failure of your life?

July 10th, 2001

Angel's Fried Erin
        Austria   Foreign Exchange
                            Student
                    Sr. year

Paula Phila. trip

Workcamp

July 23, 2001

Wright's Grandparents